Original title:
Verdure Verses

Copyright © 2025 Creative Arts Management OÜ
All rights reserved.

Author: Natalia Harrington
ISBN HARDBACK: 978-1-80566-715-5
ISBN PAPERBACK: 978-1-80566-844-2

Ode to the Dandelion

Oh dandelion, wild and bright,
You sprout in gardens, much to my fright.
A weed they claim, but what do they know?
You're sunshine hidden in grass, oh glow!

With fluffy heads that children blow,
You turn into wishes, that's quite the show!
A licorice taste—not what you'd think,
In salads or teas, you're quite the drink!

Blooming Conversations

Petunias whisper to daisies with glee,
"Why are you taller? Just grow like me!"
Roses roll their eyes, add fragrance to the chat,
"Let's all just relax and enjoy the sprat."

Sunflowers nod, trying hard to glean,
Tips on how to stay tall and green.
They laugh at the weeds creeping up in the night,
"Just let them be—what a silly sight!"

The Mosaic of Life

In gardens alive with color and cheer,
A purple radish holds onto its sphere.
A carrot chuckles, "I'm quite underground,
While you all are above, just messing around!"

Broccoli shouts, "I'm the king of the greens!
With my florets so firm, I'm not what I seem!"
But lettuce retorts, "Let's just keep it cool,
In the salad bowl, we're all just a fuel!"

Stirrings in the Greener

The grass is growing, oh what a sight!
Frogs in tuxedos are hopping with might.
Ladybugs giggle, "Is that really a bug?"
"Nope, just a beetle that's thoroughly snug."

The daisies dance with a breeze so sweet,
"Let's have a party, now that's a treat!"
While Earthworms wiggle, so sly and spry,
"Join in our dance, we're the twirlers, oh my!"

Emerald Whispers

In a garden green and bright,
The gnomes have quite a fright.
They dance and prance with glee,
While squirrels sip tea by a tree.

The flowers start to chatter loud,
As bumblebees buzz proud.
A vegetable sings a silly song,
The carrots hum along, all day long.

Green Serenade

A frog in a top hat sits,
Croaking the funkiest bits.
The daisies giggle, oh so sweet,
As they sway to the froggy beat.

The tomatoes blush, red with glee,
As beans make jokes about the sea.
A kale leaf wiggles, what a sight,
Making salad dreams at night!

Lush Corners of the Heart

In leafy nooks, where laughter grows,
A cabbage tells jokes that everyone knows.
The peas are silly, rolling about,
While the pumpkins giggle without a doubt.

The sunflowers wink, with a tall stance,
As herbs hold a wild disco dance.
A daffodil trips, slips on a root,
And the carrots all cheer, what a hoot!

The Garden's Embrace

A bouncy beet sings a cheerful song,
As lettuce joins in, they can't go wrong.
The hedgehogs jive in a melee of green,
While daisies spin, oh what a scene!

The radishes giggle, all turned in red,
Telling tales of the dreams they've bred.
A quirky thyme whispers a pun,
While the broccoli laughs, 'Oh, that was fun!'

Green Canopy Dreams

Under the trees, I took a nap,
While squirrels played an acorn trap.
A branch sneezed loud, I jumped awake,
Is nature pulling a silly prank?

Beneath green leaves, a picnic spread,
Sandwiches danced, but none were fed.
A herbivore shared my lunch too fast,
It bolted off, the first and last!

Frogs throwing parties, all in a row,
Jumps and croaks steal the show.
With lily pads, they made a stage,
Funny little critters, center-page!

So in this forest, my heart did cheer,
Nature's comedy, so very clear.
With every leaf, a laugh, a scheme,
I float away on green canopy dreams.

Nature's Tender Embrace

In the garden, plants all giggle,
A cactus laughs, it loves to wiggle.
The daisies dance, a cheerful bunch,
While butterflies wing in for lunch.

The roses tease the shy old trees,
With swaying moves, they aim to please.
A sleepy bee snoozes in bloom,
Wakes up to find it's lost its room!

Rabbits wear hats, look quite absurd,
Fashion trends in the woods quite blurred.
The sun shines down, a golden ray,
Makes all nature giggle and sway.

Amidst this green, I find my place,
In nature's tender, funny embrace.
Laughter grows from root to vine,
Each petal, leaf, is a part divine!

The Color of Renewal

Fresh sprouts giggle at morning dew,
They wear their green coats, shiny and new.
An old tree tells jokes to the breeze,
While weeds sneak in, down on their knees.

Mossy rocks hold secret goals,
They're training hard—who knows their roles?
With a chuckle, they flex and strain,
Saying, 'We're here to entertain!'

Sunflowers twist, trying to peek,
At the dancing clouds, oh so chic.
While dandelions plot and scheme,
To sprinkle wishes with a giggle and beam.

In this ruckus, all life seems bright,
Each shade of green, a comic delight.
So here's to a world, so vivid, so true,
Where the color of renewal is laughter anew!

Leafy Lullabies

Under the canopy, leaves humming low,
They sing sweet tunes as breezes blow.
A woodpecker's tap, the rhythm's set,
Nature's band, can't forget!

The bushes chuckle, making sounds,
As tiny ants march, avoiding the mounds.
They form a line—too cute for words,
Wiggle and waddle, those little nerds!

Crickets croon in the twilight hours,
Singing lullabies to blooming flowers.
While fireflies dance with flickering lights,
A fairy tale starts on warm summer nights.

In this leafy nook, dreams take flight,
Nature's lullabies, pure delight.
So close your eyes, with a grin so wide,
Let leafy whispers be your guide.

Cradle of Leaves

In the cradle of leaves, a squirrel takes a nap,
Snoring so loud, it's like a thunder clap.
While the daisies giggle, waving with glee,
'Wake up, sleepyhead, and dance with me!'

A snail in a hurry, or so he believes,
Has a plan for a race, or so he perceives.
But on a slippery path, he tumbles and slips,
With his shell as a car, he takes tiny trips.

Awakening Roots

Roots twist and twirl, like dancers at night,
Planning a ball, under the moonlight.
They hum a soft tune, with a bump and a sway,
While critters laugh loudly, in their own funky way.

A family of ants has a talent to share,
Doing a conga – without a care!
They step on each other, but never do fret,
'This party is wild, best one, I bet!'

The Pulse of the Garden

The garden's alive, it's a musical show,
With tomatoes that sing and peppers that glow.
The carrots are clapping, the onions in tears,
As they groove to the rhythm, ignoring their fears.

But watch out for weeds, with a sneaky fund,
Trying to crash the party, they think it's such fun.
The veggies unite, and they chant 'Not today!'
With a wave of their leaves, they scare them away.

Rustling Tales

In a glade filled with chatter, the winds have a tale,
Of a brave little bee, who rode on a snail.
They zoomed through the flowers, a curious pair,
Spreading sweet giggles, filling the air.

The butterflies fluttered, their wings made a fuss,
'Who's this fellow? He must be a plus!'
With a swirl and a twirl, they joined in the fun,
Sharing laughter and nectar, they shone in the sun.

The Rebirth of Flora

In the garden, blooms start to giggle,
Tiny buds dance, oh what a wiggle!
Bees in bow ties buzz with delight,
Chasing their tails, what a funny sight!

Sunflowers wear hats, oh so grand,
Waving to daisies, hand in hand.
A butterfly trips on its own wing,
In this silly garden, joy is the king!

Squirrels play tag, they leap and bound,
While mushrooms pop up from the ground.
A rabbit with glasses reads a book,
As the flowers all stop to take a look!

This floral comedy never ends,
With laughter and joy, nature transcends.
In every leaf, and every petal's swirl,
A giggle erupts in this colorful world!

Canvas of Nature's Palette.

Brushes of green paint the grass with glee,
While trees gossip sweetly, just like me.
A tulip in red, with a flair to show,
Tells jokes to the daisies, putting on a show!

Color splashes, a painter's dream,
But the clouds are just fluff, or so they seem.
Crickets play tunes with their tiny legs,
While frogs leap around, in silly pegs!

The sky throws in blues as a backdrop bright,
As the sun sneezes gold, oh what a sight!
A chameleon laughs, changing hues with ease,
Making nature's humor, a gentle tease.

This canvas alive, with laughter and cheer,
Nature's own joke, for all to hear.
Colors collide as they spin and swirl,
In this playful masterpiece, let joy unfurl!

Emerald Whisper

In the emerald woods, secrets do shuffle,
Leaves giggle softly, the trees let out a chuckle.
A hedgehog in shades sips his tea,
While the ferns gossip, as breezy as can be!

Moss grows a beard, quite wild and free,
While butterflies flutter and giggle with glee.
An owl wears a tie for the upcoming ball,
And the crickets decide to give a call!

Tall grass bows down, doing the limbo,
While curious squirrels put on a show.
Every nook and cranny, a humor spree,
In this emerald world, joy's the decree!

The whisper of green sings a funny tune,
Under the watchful eye of the moon.
In the heart of the woods, laughter runs deep,
An emerald secret, the forest keeps!

Lush Symphony

In a vibrant glade, the orchestra tunes,
While flowers hum melodies under the moons.
A frog with a baton leads the ensemble,
As a bumblebee choir begins to rumble!

The trees shake their branches to the beat,
As daisies do pirouettes on their feet.
A wind blows through, playing a soft flute,
While turtles in tuxedos dance, oh how cute!

The vines twist around, playing their part,
As laughter resounds from every heart.
In this lush concert, joy is the theme,
A symphony of nature, a whimsical dream!

As the sun sets low, the colors ignite,
A crescendo of laughter, a beautiful sight.
In the lushness of earth, where humor weaves free,
A symphonic delight, for you and for me!

Mossy Echoes of Dawn

In the early light, mossy beds lie,
Frogs croak a greeting, oh my, oh my!
A squirrel in pajamas, a nut in his hand,
Thinks he's quite ready to start a band.

The dew on the grass feels like a prank,
Slipping and sliding, I give a blank stare,
Should I dance with the daisies and do the shank?
The worms twirl back, saying, "Not a care!"

Mossy stones giggle, with secrets to share,
"Did you see that snail? He thinks he can race!"
But as he glides by, it's clear he's unaware,
Of the speedy grasshopper's winning pace.

So here's to the morning, a comical sight,
With nature's weird humor, nothing feels right!
As laughter rings out, the day starts to dawn,
In this silly ballet, we all dance along.

Petals in the Breeze

Petals pirouette in the soft, sweet wind,
Dancing like ducks, those pranksters of spring.
A ladybug winks, with a flower's best friend,
While bees buzz around like they're performing a fling.

The tulips gossip in their bright, lilac gowns,
"Did you hear what the daisies said yesterday?"
As butterflies flutter with sparkles and frowns,
One slipped in a puddle, then flew far away!

The daisies, you see, love a good old feud,
They role-play the stars in their garden disguise,
But the sun can't resist, laughs deftly ensued,
We're all just here for the sweet pastries and pies!

So spin on those petals, let laughter ensue,
With critters and blooms, there's always a show.
The breeze plays a tune, our hearts beat anew,
In this life of flowers, we'll always have glow.

Nature's Tapestry Unfurled

In woods where the squirrels strut with flair,
A tapestry sprawls, full of colors so rare.
The trees shake their leaves, play tag with the sun,
As rabbits tell jokes, oh they're having such fun.

The flowers all gossip, petals in bloom,
"Did you see that bee trip? What a comical zoom!"
Yet in the confusion, a frog leaps high,
Mistaking a puddle for a top-frog sky.

The streams start to giggle, as ripples unfold,
While fish play charades, with stories retold.
Every rock has its chuckle, its tale to impart,
In this wacky mosaic, we all play our part.

So shout from the treetops, let mirth fill the air,
With nature composing its quirky affair.
As each thread interweaves, the laughter's our guide,
In this vivid mosaic, enjoy the wild ride.

Radiant Sprouts of Hope

Tiny green sprouts, in my garden they peek,
Dare I say, they're playing hide-and-seek?
With sunlight above and giggles down low,
They plot out their strategy, putting on a show.

Down in the soil, the worms chuckle and laugh,
"With radishes racing, let's draw up a graph!"
As carrots cheer on from their cozy abode,
The radishes blush, "Can we win the gold code?"

The rain drops like fists on the thirsty ground,
And the sprouts wave their arms, making nice, silly sounds.
Each raindrop's a joke, a splash of delight,
As nature reminds us, there's joy in each fight.

So here's to the sprouts, to the laughter they share,
With petals and leaves swaying lightly in air.
In this garden of hope, there's no time for sorrow,
For every bright sprout holds a promise of tomorrow.

The Symphony of Seasons

Spring flings blooms, so bold and bright,
Summer's dance, a sunburned sight.
Autumn winks, leaves in a swirl,
Winter chuckles, snowflakes twirl.

Nature's band, a quirky show,
Every season gives us a glow.
Frogs croak tunes, and bugs hum loud,
Squirrels perform, oh, what a crowd!

Rain taps soft on leafy drums,
While flowers sway to buzzing hums.
A cactus joins, with prickly cheer,
Yelling, "Hey, I'm the star here!"

Each season plays its silly part,
In nature's dance, there's plenty of art.
So join the fun, don't be a bore,
The symphony's playing—let's explore!

Layers of Leafy Dreams

Underneath a shady tree,
Leaves whisper secrets just for me.
I hear the dreams of branches wide,
In leafy layers where giggles hide.

First a rustle, then a laugh,
A squirrel's road map to his stash.
"Forget the acorns," he shouts with glee,
"I'll eat these berries, they're fancy and free!"

The flowers gossip, petals aflutter,
"Did you see the bee? He rolled in the butter!"
Laughter erupts from vines climbing high,
"Stop the drama, darling—let's just fly!"

So in the layers, dreams abound,
Each leaf a jester, no frowns around.
In this leafy playhouse, let's all team,
And dance together in leafy dreams!

Tenderness of Roots

Beneath the soil, we wiggle and squirm,
Roots hold hands through each twist and turn.
"I'm first in line!" says the carrot sprout,
"Look at me grow, there's no doubt!"

Potatoes giggle, "We're fluffing up,
Let's dig and dance in our cozy cup!"
While onions sniffle, shedding tears,
"Don't blame us for your onion fears!"

"Keep it down, lads, we're roots of class,
With each little sprout, we bring the sass!
So plant your hopes beneath the ground,
In the tenderness of roots, joy is found!

Sunlight on Sedge

Sunbeams bounce on blades of green,
Tickling the grass—what a scene!
"Hey, don't block my rays, you clump!"
Sedge rolls over, gives a bump.

"Dance with me in this shiny glow,
Let's play chase, go to and fro!"
While daisies giggle, swaying fast,
"Catch us if you can, don't come last!"

Butterflies join the sunny spree,
Flitting about, wild and free.
With every flicker, laughter rings,
In the warmth where sunlight sings.

So join in now, feel the cheer,
With sunlight on sedge, we've nothing to fear.
Just follow the whimsy, let's have fun,
In this bright world where we all run!

Swaying Meadows and Sunlit Streams

In meadows green, the cows do dance,
With swishing tails, they take their chance.
They twirl and leap, in joy they play,
While grasshoppers chirp, hip-hip-hooray!

The sun dips low, a golden glow,
A bunny hops, then down it goes.
A splash from frogs in joyful jest,
They sing a tune, oh what a fest!

Butterflies flit on a breeze so light,
Taking selfies with the flowers bright.
While daisies giggle at the crows,
Who strut around like they own the shows!

So join the fun, don't be too sly,
In nature's realm, let laughter fly.
With swaying meadows, a sight to beam,
Life's a stage, a sunny dream!

Canopy of Tender Thoughts

Beneath the leaves, a squirrel small,
Practices stunts, to impress us all.
He jumps from branch to branch with flair,
While the wise old owl gives him a stare.

The sun peeks through, just to laugh,
At the greedy chipmunk with snacks to gaff.
He hides his treasures, thinks he's sly,
But the raccoon watches with a twinkling eye!

The wind whispers jokes that trees replay,
As branches sway in a playful way.
Acorns drop with a thud and bounce,
Like tiny bombs, they make us pounce!

In this green world, where humor grows,
Nature's comedy constantly flows.
In the canopy of thoughts so bright,
Each giggle's a flower, a pure delight!

Leafy Lullabies

Amidst the leaves, the whispers twine,
They sing of dreams with each soft line.
A ladybug joins, a cute little sprite,
Bouncing on petals, oh what a sight!

The trees sway gently, in a rhythm so sweet,
While ants march on, in formation neat.
They march to the beat of the leafy song,
With tiny trumpets, they all belong!

While shadows play, and dandelions grin,
A fox sneezes, with a comical spin.
The colors blend in a soft ballet,
As nightfall giggles, chasing day away.

So let the night sing its lullabies dear,
In the forest's charm, there's laughter near.
With leafy tunes and a giggling breeze,
Nature dances, with perfect ease!

The Art of Growing

In gardens bright, where veggies sprout,
Tomatoes blush, and so does the stout.
A cabbage rolls, what a funny sight,
While carrots giggle, oh what delight!

Dancing sprouts in a neat little row,
Making faces at rain that flows.
"Do we need sunscreen?" a radish implores,
"Don't forget hats!" the cucumber roars!

The sunflower stands, tall and proud,
While peas in pods cheer, feeling crowd.
Each petal sparkles, each leaf a star,
In the arts of growing, we've come so far!

With laughter sprouting in every nook,
Nature's canvas, a vibrant book.
Join the fun, get your green-thumb in,
For the art of life is where we begin!

A Lush Telling

In a forest where plants wear their best attire,
A cactus sings tunes as it gets a bit higher.
Lettuce tells jokes, somehow they all sprout,
While mushrooms gossip about who's going out.

The flowers all chuckle at a squirrel's brave leap,
As worms in the soil share secrets they keep.
A dandelion dreams, blowing seeds in the air,
While carrots stand still, just pretending to care.

The Grace of Vegetation

A potato waltzes, feels quite the potato,
While onions cry for no apparent reason, though.
Herbs make a band, with basil on keys,
And mint plays the drum, swaying in the breeze.

The spinach whisper secrets to old garlic cloves,
While radishes rave about daring new groves.
The kale spins a yarn, but nobody's keen,
So they laugh as it flops in its verdant sheen.

Gbrowth in Silence

A shrub without sound dreams of growing tall,
While ivy takes selfies, it's trendy after all.
The moss holds a meeting, quite plush on a stone,
Discussing the merits of being alone.

A flower with wisdom gives sage-like advice,
As a cabbage declares it's too cool to be nice.
Beets in the corner are chuckling with glee,
Imagining scenes of a leaf on a spree.

Flora's Heartbeat

The daisies are dancing, their petals all bright,
While brambles pick fights in the glow of moonlight.
Thyme has a party, invites all the greens,
While peas get clingy, just bursting at seams.

The sunflowers wave like they own the whole place,
As clovers play tag, at a quick, merry pace.
But when carrots kick back, it's a real game of stew,
With laughter that echoes, a plant comedy crew.

Garden of Echoes

In the garden where laughter grows,
Plants gossip, and everyone knows.
The daisies dance without any care,
While broccoli sings with flair!

A gnome hiccups with a red-faced glee,
As squirrels plot their grand jubilee.
Sunflowers sway to the breeze's tease,
While carrots just chill, aiming to please.

With every bump, the tomatoes giggle,
A clumsy rabbit starts to wiggle.
The peas chuckle, 'We're quite the scene!'
In this garden, all's serene!

Beneath the moon's silvery glow,
The veggies put on a funny show.
And if you listen, you just might find,
Laughter blooms, so sweet and kind.

Verdant Melodies

In fields where the greens burst with zest,
Nature's orchestra puts tunes to the test.
The broccoli plays its brave trombone,
While the lettuce serenades all alone.

Zucchini juggles, quite the display,
Beans clap along in a funky ballet.
The carrots trumpet their joyous calls,
As a busy bee stumbles, and laughs fall.

In a symphony of giggles and mirth,
The sprouts proclaim, 'We own this earth!'
While mushrooms giggle, playing hide and seek,
The kale does a two-step, oh so cheek!

As dawn appears, the chorus will rise,
The greens all dance beneath sunny skies.
With every tune, they sing out loud,
In the melody of life, they are proud.

Swaying Through Seasons

As spring arrives, the sprouts get jokes,
With every tickle, they poke at folks.
The daisies wear hats made of dew,
While squirrels dance in a fancy shoe.

Summer bounces in with a bright grin,
Where veggies play games and the fun begins.
The tomatoes hide under big leafy shields,
While the mint cheers loud from the herbal fields.

Autumn comes with a crunchy sound,
As the pumpkins giggle, rolling around.
Lettuce tells tales of leaf-blown dreams,
And the corn cackles with its golden beams.

When winter hits, they snicker and play,
Dreaming of spring's bright, joyful ballet.
In every season, they keep the cheer,
The garden's giggles, both far and near.

Green Reverie

In a world painted green, oh what a sight,
Where laughter blooms in the morning light.
The cucumbers whisper, 'Let's start a band!'
While radishes plot with their little green stand.

Spinach wears glasses and reads the news,
While peppers try handstands in their crazy shoes.
The radishes yell, 'We'll produce a show!'
As the herbs coo softly, just letting it flow.

In a patch of greens, the fun never ends,
As broccoli breaks dancing, hoping to trend.
The carrots exchange silly little quips,
While squash gives the globe a few cheeky flips.

At dusk they gather, all in a line,
Sharing tall tales of the best vine.
In this green reverie, there's laughter loud,
A quirky kingdom of veggies proud.

The Sylvan Symphony

In a forest full of trees,
Squirrels dance upon the leaves,
A chorus of chirps and squeaks,
Nature's band plays as it weaves.

Frogs croak with a whimsical tune,
While raccoons tap their little feet,
A bear joins in, oh what a boon,
Making this concert quite the treat.

Breezes tickle grassy blades,
As flowers join, they sway and twirl,
Dancing to their leafy grades,
Spreading joy in nature's whirl.

The sun peeks through the leafy stars,
As owls hoot out some solid jokes,
While fireflies twinkle near and far,
A night of giggles and wise folks.

Sprig of Dreams

Once a sprig thought it could fly,
Tied a kite to a twig so spry,
But the kite went up in a sigh,
And sprig just chuckled, oh my, oh my!

Frogs believed they could leap the moon,
Practiced a jump with a grand swoon,
But instead they plopped in a lagoon,
And laughed till dawn, a silly tune.

A rabbit wore a hat so tall,
Claimed it made him best of all,
But when he tripped and took a fall,
The flowers cheered, "You've got style, after all!"

In this place where dreams expand,
Joy's the rule, with jest at hand,
Nature's giggle, a funny band,
Sprouting smiles across the land.

Flourishing under the Sky

Dandelions declared a race,
To see who'd reach the highest space,
But one got caught in a cat's face,
And laughter echoed, oh what a chase!

Bees buzzing with ego in flight,
Swore they'd out-pollinate all night,
But slipped on nectar; what a sight,
Tangled up in their own delight.

A bumblebee wore a tiny crown,
Strutting as if he owned the town,
But with a slip, he tumbled down,
"Oh well," he buzzed, "I'll bounce around!"

Under blossoms, the laughter grew,
Every tickle, every breeze blew,
Nature's giggles, a vibrant view,
Flourishing joy, a merry crew.

In the Shade of Ancient Trees

In the shade of trees, a bird sings,
Claiming it knew all the best things,
But its knowledge was quite the fling,
Mistaking worms for diamond rings!

A wise old owl had much to share,
But fell asleep while sitting there,
Told dreams of jokes beyond compare,
Leaving all critters in wild despair.

Chipmunks debated the best snack,
Almonds or berries, what's the knack?
But both got buried, what a whack,
Nutty for snacks, the forest's track!

In this realm where thoughts run free,
Laughter echoes from every tree,
With silliness as a decree,
The shade holds wisdom, jokes, and glee!

Colorful Fragments of Life

In the garden where daisies dance,
Bees bounce around in a silly prance.
A butterfly flops, oh what a sight,
Trying to land, but it takes flight.

Roses giggle, thorns feel shy,
Tulips whisper, 'Oh me, oh my!'
Sunflowers look up with a grin,
While dandelions puff and begin to spin.

A worm with glasses reads the news,
While ants debate in fancy shoes.
Ladybugs waltz, all in a line,
This garden's a party, in the sun they shine.

Even the weeds want to be a part,
Claiming their space with all of their heart.
It's a riot of color, a lovely spree,
Life's blooming laughter, wild and free.

Beneath the Green Canopy

Underneath the leafy spread,
Squirrels chatter, making their bed.
A raccoon peeks with a curious stare,
As if it's planning, a woodland fair!

Trees exchange jokes, their branches sway,
Wind tickles leaves in a playful way.
A wise old owl spins tales at night,
With a wink, it puts the stars in fright!

The brook laughs with every splash,
Frogs join in with a jumping crash.
Mice wear hats made of grass and dew,
To start a dance, just me and you!

In this patch, the fun never halts,
Nature's a comedy, with no default.
Striped mushrooms cheer with a soft delight,
Beneath this canopy, all feels right!

Nature's Quiet Revelations

Morning dew, a crystal tease,
Brings out the giggles in the breeze.
Clouds parade, fluffy and wise,
Acting like sheep, in sunny skies.

A chipmunk juggles acorns with flair,
While grasshoppers hop without a care.
The sun peeks out, makes mischief today,
While shadows play hide-and-seek in the hay.

Butterflies borrow colors that shine,
Each one boasts, "Look, this hue is mine!"
The earth chuckles with a gentle sigh,
As blooms pop up, just to say hi.

In this space, where laughter grows,
A ticklish tickle in the warm cosmos.
Nature whispers secrets, wrapped in fun,
Revealing joys, under the sun!

Roots of Reflection

Beneath the soil, the roots have flair,
They throw a party, with dirt in their hair.
Napping worms are juggling with dreams,
Planning a feast with underground themes.

The trees share gossip, whisper with might,
"Did you hear about that squirrel last night?"
Leaves high five as the wind takes a spin,
In this rooty realm, every laugh's a win!

Rocks tell stories of ages gone by,
With crickets crooning an old lullaby.
Moss wears a cape, such charming style,
While the soil laughs, oh, what a mile!

In this deep earth, reflections do bloom,
Every giggle lifts away the gloom.
Roots and shoots, they cheer and connect,
Life's hidden humor, the best architect!

Skylark Serenade

A skylark sings with such great flair,
While landing clumsily in midair.
It trips on petals, what a sight!
Then bounces back, ready for flight.

The daisies giggle, swaying in time,
Each one thinks it's a poet sublime.
They dance and twirl, a floral spree,
While trying to steal the bird's jamboree.

On and on, the melody soars,
Till someone sneezes, oh what a wars!
The pollen flies, a comical scene,
Nature's own whimsical routine!

So let us join this jovial crew,
With silly moves, a laugh or two.
For in the garden, the joy is clear,
A serenade of laughter each year.

The Flourishing Grove

In a grove where the trees play peek-a-boo,
Squirrels debate, which nut is due?
The oak says, 'Mine is the biggest!',
While the willow just squeaks, ever so briskest.

The mushrooms gather for a big feast,
Planning a party, but don't invite the yeast!
They dance on roots, with twirls and spins,
Till the owl arrives, and the giggling begins.

The hedgehogs wear hats for the grand show,
While rabbits jump in, stealing the glow.
They tumble and roll, a chaotic blend,
A garden party that won't ever end!

So if you're down, come join this crew,
In the flourishing grove, there's fun for you.
With laughter and joy, it's a vibrant place,
A silly escape, nature's embrace.

Petal Poetry

Petals scribble words in the breeze,
Crafting verses with such playful ease.
The tulips blush and the roses grin,
As dandelions drift, they wear a win.

A ladybug writes on a leaf so fine,
While ants debate if winter is divine.
They argue and shout, with a comic bite,
'Till the sun sets, we'll keep up the fight!'

With flavors of laughter, they rotely rhyme,
Each bloom a comedian, passing the time.
The violets giggle at every pun,
In this patch of humor, we all have fun!

So gather round for the petal discourse,
Where flowers jest with charming course.
In this garden of whimsy, come lose your woes,
For it's the silliest show that nature chose!

A Glimpse of Green

In the park, grass wears a grin,
Squirrels dance, they spin and spin.
A picnic spread, ants form a line,
They're planning lunch, oh isn't that divine?

Frisbees fly, like birds they roam,
Chasing shadows, far from home.
A muddy shoe tells tales of woe,
How did it end in a splashy show?

Lions in yards, well, kinda not,
Lawn gnomes guarding a barbecue lot.
Laughter echoes under the sun,
While the dog plots a sneaky run.

Backyard jungles grow wild with pride,
Mom's yelling "Keep it off the slide!"
Nature's playground is such a tease,
Where fun unfolds with the rustling leaves.

The Poetic Grove

In the grove, trees have jokes to share,
Whispering secrets in the warm, sweet air.
Barking dogs roll in the grass,
As squirrels wear acorns as a clever glass.

A bumblebee serves a buzzing tune,
While daisies giggle at the bright full moon.
The old oak tree waves its leafy arms,
Saying, "Watch out for nature's charms!"

Raccoons sneak snacks from lunchboxes near,
While picnickers laugh, joy's atmosphere.
Oh look, there's a rogue sandwich on the ground,
Nature's buffet, to the delight of hounds!

In this grove, humor blooms so free,
Even the shrubs share smirks of glee.
Each branch and bush plays its part,
Nature's comedy, a serene work of art.

Wildflowers' Secret Songs

In fields of color, wildflowers play,
Singing softly on a breezy day.
A bumblebee wearing stripes so bright,
Swears it's the disco king of the night!

Petunias gossip, "Look at that bee!"
With floppy a petal, it dances with glee.
Butterflies flit in a dazzling dance,
As flowers whisper, "Give us a chance!"

Beneath the daisies, frogs hold a show,
Croaking tunes to an audience below.
They ribbit and hop, like a "dance-off" spree,
Making wild tales from the roots of a tree.

Every wild bloom has a tale to spin,
Of sunshine, rain, and the laughs within.
Nature's humor graces every stem,
With wildflowers giggling—a raucous anthem!

Boughs of Joy

Boughs sway gently, like old friends at play,
Telling stories in a breezy café.
"Hey, did you hear?" the willow replies,
"I sold my leaves to the squirrels for fries!"

Bamboo blades chuckle, their rhythm divine,
As coyotes sing while sipping on wine.
Branches hold secrets, they twirl and bend,
In this forest dance, with laughter to send.

A rabbit hops in, and what a sight,
Decked in a hat, it's quite a delight!
"Join the fun!" it shouts with a skip,
While birds tweet in harmony, lost in the trip.

Under these boughs, joy dances around,
With chirps and giggles, a whimsical sound.
Nature's funny side takes us away,
In the shade, where the boughs laugh and play.

The Green Whisper

In the garden, a leaf did blab,
Telling tales of a wandering crab.
Uh-oh, said the flower, that's too much!
Keep it quiet, we're not one to touch!

Worms are gossiping beneath the dirt,
They talk of roots and the mighty shirt.
Grasshoppers leap, with a chuckle and sway,
Plant jokes fly, what a leafy play!

Echoes of Spring

A bird with style, in a snazzy blue,
Sways to the rhythm, oh, what a view!
The daisies chuckle, heads held high,
While bees break dance, buzzing by.

A sneaky snail slips, in a stylish glide,
Wears a shell that he takes with pride.
The ants all cheer for their champion slow,
"Who needs a race? Let's take it nice and slow!"

Nature's Gentle Palette

In the meadow, colors swirl and dance,
A flower's pink seems to prance by chance.
Butterflies giggle, adorned with flair,
"Who wore it best? Just look at that pair!"

The sun throws confetti, golden and bright,
Painting the clouds with smiles of delight.
The trees high-five as the breezes twirl,
"Life's a canvas, let's give it a whirl!"

Freshly Turned Soil

Digging deep, with a twist and a shout,
The dirt reveals treasures, there's no doubt.
A carrot sighs, "I'm all snug down here,
Do I really have to face the light? Oh dear!"

Moles hold a meeting, underground fame,
Discussing their digs, it's a serious game.
"Who found the best worms?" they eagerly cheer,
As the roots giggle, just wishing for beer!

Blossom's Melodic Dance

In the spring, the flowers whirled,
A daisy tripped on its own little curl,
Tulips danced a jig, oh what a sight,
While sunflowers sang with all their might.

The bees joined in with a buzzing tone,
They made a trio, and laughed alone,
A butterfly slipped in, trying its best,
But tangled in petals, it failed the test.

A garden gnome laughed, sipping on tea,
Watching the chaos while under a tree,
"Just don't step on me!" he yelled with glee,
As the tune of nature played merrily.

With each bow and sway, the petals flew,
Mixing colors, like a painter's brew,
The joy of bloom, in their cheeky prance,
Echoed loudly in Blossom's dance.

Sylvan Rhapsody

In the glade where the squirrels conspire,
A mischief brewed around the fire,
The trees were grooving, swaying to tune,
While raccoons played spoons beneath the moon.

A parrot squawked, "Let's sing a rhyme!"
Then tripped on a branch, oh what a crime!
The owls hooted in a chuckling way,
As the party raged till the break of day.

With mossy rugs and a ferny spread,
They dined on acorns and slices of bread,
A hedgehog in shades declared with flair,
"Join in the fun! There's magic in air!"

As laughter echoed through leaves so green,
In this whimsical world, joy was seen,
Under the sun, they danced with glee,
A symphony played by nature's spree.

The Garden's Secret Song

There's a tune in the garden, if you can hear,
It's sung by the carrots, quite far and near,
With a rhythm of roots and a beat of the soil,
"Let's wiggle and jiggle, oh let's make it royal!"

The radishes blushed, with leafy greens,
Spinning around like they're in dream scenes,
While the peppers salsa danced with pride,
They twirled and they whirled, side by side.

"Tomatoes, you're saucy!" the onions cried loud,
Their laughter was mixed in a veggie crowd,
A zucchini tapped toes, quite on its own,
While the pumpkins bobbed to the joyous tone.

Through the rows the giggles fluttered,
With every surprise, a seed had muttered,
In the garden's embrace, the song echoed strong,
A silly parade, where everything's wrong!

Foliage's Gentle Caress

The leaves swayed gently, their whispering cheer,
Tickling each other as they drew near,
"Hey, watch me glide!" said a leaf with a grin,
And fell to the ground with a most epic spin.

"Did you see that?" shouted a brazen old bark,
While acorns laughed, lighting up the park,
"Let's tumble and tumble, no time to be tame,
We're the wildlings here, no one's to blame!"

A breeze slipped through with a cheeky nudge,
Pushing the petals to dance and judge,
"Stop limping, you stems! It's a wild leaf frolic,
Let's make some noise, it's time for a colic!"

With chuckles and jiggles, the foliage played,
Creating a ruckus beside a cool glade,
Under sunbeams, they twirled and swayed,
In this charming chaos, all worries delayed.

Dappled Light and Shadow

In a garden where shadows play,
The daisies giggle, come what may.
Sunbeams dance with a cheeky grin,
While squirrels organize a tambourine.

The trees wear hats of leafy greens,
And whisper secrets through the scenes.
A gnome steals cookies from a plate,
While ladybugs debate their fate.

A butterfly wearing polka dots,
Plays hide and seek with the pesky ants.
The flowers burst in raucous cheer,
As bees buzz jokes for all to hear.

Amidst the laughter and delight,
The sun dips low, goodbye, goodnight.
Yet dreams of greens will surely stay,
In this whimsical, wild ballet.

Earth's Fresh Refrain

In the meadow, grass sings loud,
With cows mooing, feeling proud.
A chicken struts in fancy shoes,
While frogs audition for the blues.

The daisies shout, 'Look at me!'
While crickets play the harmony.
A worm holds tight on a disco floor,
Twisting and turning, wanting more.

Rabbits hop with a silly flair,
Chasing clouds without a care.
They tumble down on clover beds,
While bees debate their sleepy heads.

As dusk arrives, the critters hum,
A lullaby for all for fun.
In every nook and every lane,
The Earth hums forth its fresh refrain.

Kingdom of Flora

Welcome to the kingdom fair,
Where tulips dance without a care.
The petunias wear their brightest hues,
And span their petals to amuse.

The weeds throw parties in a row,
While garden gnomes put on a show.
A hedgehog juggles shiny stones,
While fragrant jasmine sings soft moans.

Sunflowers stand like guards so tall,
Demanding respect from one and all.
But in a corner, hidden tight,
A cactus rolls, and joins the fight.

At twilight's close, the flora beams,
In this kingdom of giggles and dreams.
With every rustle, every cheer,
The flowers whisper, 'We're glad you're here!'

Gardens of Tranquility

In the gardens where calm blossoms flow,
A turtle draws lines in the soft, pure snow.
The roses recite their favorite joke,
While a playful breeze gives a gentle poke.

Fish swim in puddles, planning their pranks,
While daisies strategize their flowered ranks.
A butterfly flutters with giggles in pairs,
Fashionista in style, it combs its bright hairs.

The rhododendrons chime, 'Life is a breeze!'
While ferns sway softly, sizzling with ease.
An owl pops in to narrate a tale,
Of how chips fell off an old wooden rail.

As evening drifts softly, a cricket takes lead,
With a song laced in humor, for all that we need.
In these gardens of laughter, our troubles will flee,
With nature's own giggles, forever carefree.

Shaded Soliloquy

In the shade, I saw a mouse,
Wearing a tiny little blouse.
It danced around, quite a sight,
Chasing shadows left and right.

Beneath the leaves, I took a seat,
A squirrel claimed my snack to eat.
I laughed out loud, what a surprise,
To see his clever, twinkling eyes.

The flowers giggle in the breeze,
While leaves engage in silly tease.
A grasshopper joined in the fun,
Jumping high, kissing the sun.

In this green world, laughter grows,
A party where everyone knows.
With nature's quirks, we can all say,
Life's a hoot in a leafy way.

Vibrant Earth's Embrace

In the garden, sprouts did sprout,
But one was busy playing doubt.
A cabbage said, 'Just take the chance!'
While radishes started to dance.

Tomatoes burst with juicy pride,
As pumpkins rolled with laughter wide.
They joked of rain and sunshine's play,
How mud pies made for a fun day.

The herbs were gossiping with glee,
While beans climbed high to see the spree.
Each carrot told a corny pun,
That made the lettuce laugh and run.

In this patch, all colors blend,
With every leaf, a prank to send.
Nature's stage where jesters bloom,
In earthy fun, we find our room.

Whispers of the Wild

The trees conspire, what a sight,
To pull a prank at dawn's first light.
A bird with style wore a hat,
While deer exchanged their tales of spat.

With whispered jokes beneath the boughs,
A raccoon slept, but snored like cows.
The flowers blushed at playful tease,
As butterflies teased with a breeze.

A bear showed up for open mic,
His growl was more of a shy bike.
With jokes that made the owls roll eyes,
Even the stone-faced rocks would rise!

In nature's laughter, echoes clear,
The whispers of the wild we hear.
A symphony of joyful cheer,
Where every critter draws us near.

The Secrets of Greenery

In tangled vines, the secrets lay,
Of how to make a perfect play.
The ferns discussed their strategies,
As dandelions shared the keys.

A wise old oak perched up so tall,
Told of the best leaf-dance of all.
While mushrooms giggled on the ground,
As grassy jokes swirled all around.

The ivy climbed with stealthy grace,
To reach the laughter's vibrant place.
A beetle hummed an upbeat tune,
As sunbeams chuckled with the moon.

Every leaf had a tale to tell,
Of sneaky antics and how to dwell.
In secrets found where plants convene,
Life thrives funny in shades of green.

The Birth of a Leaf

A sprout breaks ground, it starts to sneeze,
Out pops a green with the greatest of ease.
"I'm fashionably late!" it calls with glee,
While sunbeams giggle, "Oh, look at he!"

The breeze gives a laugh, blowing to and fro,
"You'll need a hat!" says a daisy, aglow.
"A leaf without style? That's quite a faux pas!"
"But I'm just a baby, I don't know the law!"

The garden erupts into joyful jeers,
As ladybugs count all the new growth peers.
"You'll grow in time, just wait and see!"
Then all join the dance, so wild and free!

Finally a swirl, our leaf takes flight,
"Hello, little world! It's a glorious sight!"
With each little nod, the green cheer spills,
As seedlings giggle and sunlight thrills.

Aria of the Meadow

In a meadow so plump, a butterfly's glowed,
"I can sing like a pro!" on the daisies it strode.
"Dance with me, flowers! Let's start a big show!"
But the daisies just chuckled, "You've made quite a grow!"

Little ants marched in, with a tune so bold,
"We're here for the party, so let's break the mold!"
But the grass raised its blades, with suspense in the air,
"No stomping, please! We know how to flair!"

Wiggling worms joined, in sequined attire,
"We're the foundation, your moves inspire!"
While the clouds overhead made their shadows cast,
"We're here to rain fun, let's forget the past!"

The sun laughed aloud, with a warm, golden grin,
"You all seem quite jolly! Let the fun begin!"
With laughter and dance, all agreed with a cheer,
In the meadow of mishaps, friendship is near.

In the Shade of the Oaks

Under oaks so mighty, a snail in a shell,
"I'm quite the explorer, won't you ring my bell?"
The shadows reply, with a rustling sigh,
"Keep snail mail slow—don't rush or you'll fry!"

A squirrel zipped by, hoarding nuts so spry,
"You think you can challenge my snack game? Oh why!"
The snail rolled its eyes, with a grin not so sweet,
"I'm a gourmet chef! Just can't handle the heat!"

A chorus of crickets, their tunes all a buzz,
"Let's form a band, we'll play just because!"
But the oak groaned low, "Please keep it down sound,
You're shaking my leaves, and that isn't so profound!"

With raucous giggles, they finished their jam,
As the sun set low, casting shadows so grand.
In the shade of the oaks, what a sight to behold,
Friendship over snacks, worth its weight in gold!

The Kingdom Beneath

Deep in the soil, where the critters dwell,
A council met up, with secrets to sell.
"Who rules this realm?" asked a curious worm,
"It's the ants with their marches, they've taken the term!"

A mole wearing glasses proclaimed, with a grin,
"But we dig the best tunnels; let the fun begin!"
A rabbit chimed in, "I hop so much faster,
Those ants need a map; they're just a disaster!"

Each critter debated, with chuckles and cheer,
"We need an ambassador! Make sure it's sincere!"
A wise frog offered, "I'll croak up a plan,
We'll have a party; let all know we can!"

Invitations were sent, to all the small homes,
And critters came hopping, while ants brought their gnomes.
In the kingdom below, oh what a delight,
They danced and they laughed, till they lost track of night!

Petals in the Breeze

Petals dance with glee, so free,
They tip their hats to me, you see!
A butterfly winks, so much to say,
While dandelions giggle, come what may.

The flowers play tag, what a sight!
With bees buzzing in sheer delight.
They sip sweet nectar, oh so bold,
In this garden's secrets, tales unfold.

Grasshoppers leap, they're quite the champs,
While worms wiggle, throwing tiny prams.
A ladybug's blushing, red on green,
In this blooming circus, a playful scene.

Laughter fills the air, so bright,
As nature stages her silly sight.
With a whiff of mint, fun's in the air,
In this whimsical realm, without a care.

A Tapestry of Growth

In the garden, things are sprouting,
With tomatoes laughing, there's no doubting.
Zucchini sings a silly tune,
While carrots dance beneath the moon.

The cucumbers wear hats, so grand,
As melons hold hands, oh isn't it planned!
Sunflowers wink with a golden heart,
In this playful patch, nature's art.

Pumpkins roll with a goofy grin,
Sharing secrets of how they win.
Basil whispers, 'I'm here for tea!'
While peppers join in, spicy and free.

Every sprout brings a twist of cheer,
In this veggie world, no room for fear.
Nature's joke is a delightful riff,
In this tapestry, every plant's a gift.

The Sound of Budding Life

In the hush of dawn, a rustle stirs,
As flowers wake and shake their furs.
Chirping birds hold a morning chat,
While squirrels prance in an acorn spat.

Leaves whisper secrets in the breeze,
While frogs croak tunes that aim to please.
A snail's slow race, oh what a sight,
As ladybugs take off in flight.

Roots are dancing beneath the ground,
While ants march in a silly round.
A pebble sings of its stony plight,
In this budding life, everything's bright!

Sunrise spills gold upon each leaf,
As laughter blooms, beyond belief.
Nature's orchestra is quite a show,
With every sound, a punchline to glow.

Sylvan Sojourn

In leaves' embrace, where laughter thrives,
The trees tell tales of their busy lives.
A goat struts past with a jaunty air,
While chipmunks giggle without a care.

Squirrels debate 'bout acorn finds,
While raccoons plot mischief, very unkind.
A woodpecker taps a cheeky beat,
As mushrooms chuckle underfoot discreet.

The brook gurgles jokes of wet delight,
Reflecting sunbeams both warm and bright.
Frogs leap on stage in a slimy play,
In this sylvan world, fun leads the way.

Nature's dance is a whimsical spree,
Where every nook holds a mystery.
In this leafy realm, laughter unfurls,
As woodland critters share their twirls.

The Dance of the Wildflowers

In fields where daisies spin and sway,
A bumblebee joins in the ballet.
With petals bright, they giggle and twirl,
While butterflies twinkling, give it a whirl.

The daisies whisper, "Watch us prance!"
With wind as their partner, they laugh and dance.
But oh, the poor tulips, stuck in a row,
With arms too short to join the show.

Sunflowers nod, all big and tall,
While clovers chime in, "We're having a ball!"
And as the rain starts to sprinkle down,
The wildflowers slip—who's wearing the crown?

So join the frolic, don't miss your chance,
In gardens of giggles, let's all dance!
For flowers and friends, it's no boring fate—
Just watch out for bees who might overate!

Subtle Shades of Life

In shades of green where squirrels play,
The leaves gossip about the day.
"Did you see that cat? On my branch he sat!"
"Oh please, that's nothing—see how I acrobat?"

Frogs croak jokes by the lily pads,
While turtles roll eyes, all green and glad.
"Life's a splash! Let's leap and glide!"
"Oh no, not again, I'm taking a ride."

The colors are subtle but surely cheeky,
As daisies claim, "We are quite freaky!"
With ladybugs buzzing, "We're here for flair!"
Each hue in the garden has a story to share.

So watch how the breezes tickle the trees,
Where laughter and whispers ride on the breeze.
Under the sun, it's a vibrant scene—
With all the jests in the spaces between!

Canopy Chronicles

In the treetops, the stories unfold,
From owls in nightcaps to squirrels so bold.
They gossip about who steals the best nuts,
While wise old trees go: "Oh dear, what a ruts!"

The sunlight giggles through leaves hung low,
As a raccoon in pajamas puts on a show.
With acorns as props, he's stealing the scene,
While birds in a choir belt out their routine.

Beneath the canopy, a fruit bat lies,
Snoring so loudly, through tangled vines.
"Was that a nap, or a comedy act?"
All creatures agree, it's a true forest fact!

So gather your tales under branches so grand,
Where laughter and whispers go hand in hand.
Each leaf shares a secret in light or in dark,
With nature's own giggles and a little heart spark!

Verdant Inspirations

In lush green fields where ideas sprout,
The grass whispers secrets, without a doubt.
"Let's make a hat from clover and leaves!"
"And I'll fashion boots from the bark of the thieves!"

The flowers debate on colors so bright,
"Who wore it best? Let's have a fight!"
A poppy winks, "I'm redder by far!"
While daisies giggle, "We're all bizarre!"

The breeze brings tales from the garden's embrace,
Of insects in suits plotting a race.
"Let's build a rocket of seeds and of twigs!"
"Can't wait to meet Martians—the funny old figs!"

So sip on the dew from the morning light,
The world's filled with laughter, nature's delight.
With each fun notion that springs up anew,
In a garden of whimsy, there's always room for two!

Nurtured Dreams

In a garden of whimsy, plants chat all day,
The carrots are gossiping in a silly way.
Tomatoes are blushing, their cheeks a bright red,
While cucumbers giggle, 'Aren't we well-fed?'

The daisies are dancing in a breeze that is light,
While sunflowers play peekaboo, oh what a sight!
They poke out their heads, then duck down with glee,
'We're the stars of this show, just you wait and see!'

A worm with a top hat gives a speech to the beans,
'We'll grow to be legends, if you know what I mean!'
But the peas just roll laughter, they burst at the seams,
'In our world of green dreams, who needs fancy themes?'

As twilight approaches, the plants settle in,
With whispers of laughter, let the fun begin!
For every small sprout has a tale to convey,
In this world of green antics, let's play every day!

The Overture of Earth

The grass played a tune with a tickle and wiggle,
While daisies hummed softly, just a touch of a giggle.
The oak tree swayed gently, a conductor so wise,
And ants marched in rhythm with snacks for their prize.

Bees buzzed like trumpets, all fluffed up and proud,
While butterflies fluttered, draped in colors loud.
The earthworm on drums kept the beat with great flair,
'Let's rock this whole meadow, we'll fill the fresh air!'

The rain joined the chorus with pitter-pat beats,
Creating a symphony of nature's sweet treats.
The clouds overhead chimed in, fluffy and bright,
'Let's jam on this stage until we're out of sight!'

As dusk turned to night, the stars twinkled bright,
The overture ended, but oh, what a sight!
With fireflies sparkling, a nightcap at hand,
Nature's wild concert, a cheer for the land!

The Rhythms of Renewal

In springtime's grand dance, flowers twirl with delight,
The tulips wear tutus, what a colorful sight!
The violets are giggling, 'Look at us go!'
While lilacs croon softly, 'We steal every show!'

The raindrops have rhythm, like feet on a floor,
While the sun throws in laughter, 'Let's dance it some more!'
The breezes play tricks, tangle hair in a knot,
As leaves start a shuffle, in a lively plot.

The caterpillars wiggle, they're groovy and bold,
Dreaming of wings as their stories unfold.
'Let's boogie, my friends, we'll rise high and free,
From a fuzzy green caterpillar to a butterfly spree!'

With a spin and a leap, the season takes flight,
Adding layers of laughter to day and to night.
Nature's great waltz, it's a hilarious tease,
Where every new cycle brings joy with such ease!

Nature's Palette

A painter with shades, the world is their song,
With brushes of blossoms, they paint all day long.
The blue of the sky, mixed with grass's bright hue,
'Let's splash on some daisies, and maybe a few!'

The rivers run wild, like a playful cascade,
While rocks stand like models, perfectly laid.
Clouds dabble in white, like frosting on cakes,
And rainbows throw parties when the sunshine awakes.

The trees wear their leaves like a fashionable dress,
While squirrels, in mockery, show off their finesse.
With each stroke of nature, a story unfolds,
A canvas of laughter, filled with colors so bold.

At dusk, the horizon blazes orange and pink,
While critters below share a winking blink.
In this vibrant display, creativity flows,
Nature's great artwork, everybody bestows!

Nature's Harmonious Breath

In the meadow, cows dance on lace,
Frogs croon tunes in a wobbly embrace.
Leaves gossip secrets, a rustling affair,
While squirrels play tag, without a care.

A daisied sun winks, in a silly way,
Tickling the grass blades that twirl and sway.
Bumblebees buzz, filling the air,
Their clumsy ballet, a stage quite rare.

The wind throws a party, with a whoosh and a whirl,
Inviting all critters, both swine and girl.
Upon the old stump, mice hold a ball,
As nature chuckles, keeping spirits tall.

Every flower blushes, the colors ignite,
With petals so vibrant, it's quite a sight.
Nature's chuckle lingers, a sweet little jest,
As laughter blooms on this merry quest.

Symphony of New Beginnings

Amidst the flowers, chickens prance,
Their fluffy feathers in a funny dance.
Worms whisper tunes to the beetle brigade,
As ants do the tango, quite unafraid.

Sprouts spring forth, all green and bright,
Silly seedlings reach for the warm sunlight.
The sun grins down, a big golden ball,
While clouds play hide and seek, having a ball.

Buds unfold, eager as can be,
As butterflies flutter, what a sight to see!
A ladybug laughs with a humorous wink,
Chasing around bees, as they share a drink.

Mother Nature plays a mischievous game,
With rabbits and foxes, it's never the same.
Each dawn marks a joke, so light and spry,
In the symphony of life, all creatures comply.

Flourish in Harmony

In vibrant gardens where chaos blends,
The carrots and radishes call each other friends.
They gossip over soil in fun little rhymes,
While singing sweet tunes about sunny times.

Bees wear their buzz like a fuzzy hat,
While a cat tries to catch them, imagine that!
Lettuce just giggles as it sways in the breeze,
Chortling at capers of squirrels in the trees.

The daisies are decked in polka-dot gowns,
As daisies debate who wears the best crowns.
With every green leaf, the laughter expands,
As nature orchestrates with funny little hands.

Pansies are winking, the sun's in on the joke,
While tomatoes roll down, a soft, squishy poke.
Each day in this patch is a joyous song,
Where woes of the world never really belong.

Essence of the Forest

In the heart of the woods, where the giggles grow,
    Mushrooms sport hats, it's quite the show!
Trees sway and shimmy, their branches a mess,
As pine cones drop down, making quite the stress.

    Owls hoot in laughter, their jokes fly high,
        While rabbits race by, quick as a sigh.
    The brook bubbles over with silly delight,
        Whispering secrets to stars in the night.

With daffodils smirking and ferns all amused,
    The forest is vibrant, refreshingly used.
    As critters embrace in a jovial dance,
Life in the woods gives whimsy a chance.

    So come and join in this humorous tale,
        Where nature's oddities never do fail.
In the essence of life, let the laughter resound,
    For happiness blooms on this playful ground.

www.ingramcontent.com/pod-product-compliance
Lightning Source LLC
Chambersburg PA
CBHW051634160426
43209CB00004B/649